TypeScript
Crash Course
for Beginners

Greg Lim

Table of Contents

Preface

In this book, we take you on a fun, hands-on crash course to learning TypeScript. TypeScript is one of the most important tools for JavaScript developers. But some avoid it thinking that it is a chore to have squiggly red lines appear in their code. This practical guide shows how TypeScript actually makes your code better and makes you think like a senior developer.

In the course of this book, we will cover:
- Transiting to TypeScript
- Defensive Coding
- Types, Defining Custom Types and Nested Object Types
- Optional Properties
- Unions
- Type Narrowing
- Should we use *Any*
- Utility Types - Partial and Omit
- Generics and their Application

and more.

The goal of this book is to teach you TypeScript in a manageable way without overwhelming you. We focus only on the essentials and cover the material in a hands-on practice manner for you to code along.

Getting Book Updates

To receive updated versions of the book, subscribe to our mailing list by sending a mail to support@i-ducate.com. I try to update my books to use the latest version of software, libraries and will update the codes/content in this book. So do subscribe to my list to receive updated copies!

Contact and Code Examples

Contact me at support@i-ducate.com to obtain the source files used in this book. Comments or questions concerning this book can also be directed to the same.

Chapter 1: Introduction

Welcome to this introductory book on TypeScript. But why learn Typescript? Three of the most important reasons for learning TypeScript are:
- Enhanced Code Quality
- Improved Developer Productivity
- Growing Popularity

Enhanced Code Quality

TypeScript's ability to check your code during compile time (or using modern IDEs, essentially in real-time as you type your code), dramatically reduces the number of app-crashing runtime errors that would normally be caught only after your app is deployed. Because TypeScript can catch a lot of those errors before anything gets pushed live, you as a developer have confidence in the stability of your code.

Improved Developer Productivity

TypeScript increases productivity as a developer. Yes, TypeScript takes a bit more time to write than regular JavaScript code, but it has a number of neat features that make it easier for developers.

Modern TypeScript-enabled IDEs have better autocomplete, refactoring capabilities, immediate error checking (we discussed this earlier), and other features you'll find as you're using TypeScript that significantly improves your developer experience and productivity.

Growing Popularity

Thirdly, learning TypeScript improves employability because it is increasingly adopted in the industry, especially for larger projects. Many prominent companies, such as Microsoft, Google, Notion, Slack, Figma, Palantir, and many others, use TypeScript in their projects. It is used in popular frameworks like Angular and supported by React and Vue. In fact, I have written a book on Angular using TypeScript (contact support@i-ducate for a free copy).

What will we cover in this book?

This is an introductory book. We break down topics into bite-sized chunks that are easy to comprehend. By the end, you will understand the fundamentals of TypeScript, and why TypeScript is so useful.

We're going to cover
- basic, literal, and custom types
- optional properties,
- Unions,
- type narrowing,
- built-in Utility types that exist in TypeScript, and
- Generics to make your functions and other types more flexible.

Understanding these Typescript fundamentals helps train your thinking process to be like that of a senior developer.

Is TypeScript Extra Work?

One of the challenges of learning TypeScript is it feels like extra work without additional benefits. Especially if you try to convert an existing codebase into TypeScript, it is overwhelming to see errors pop up when you change your file to a TypeScript one.

But TypeScript doesn't make one's code terrible. It simply shows how horrible the code already is. The errors in TypeScript are not there to annoy you. They are there to protect you against some loose and careless typing that happens in vanilla JavaScript. The errors that TypeScript identifies can save you big headaches later on, especially in production.

Now, TypeScript only solves some programming problems. The main focus of TypeScript is fixing possible runtime errors. More specifically, anything that would be a type error (hence the name TypeScript).

Not every code error is a runtime-type error. TypeScript can protect you against the most common errors people write in their JavaScript code, but it won't protect you against logical errors.

That said, we will see how many errors we can fix by changing a file from a JavaScript extension to a TypeScript extension.

Chapter 2: Introduction to Library App

When you first start learning TypeScript, you might need help understanding the benefits of using TypeScript instead of plain JavaScript. Indeed, writing code in TypeScript requires an overhead in writing extra lines of code and considerations.

Thus, we want to demonstrate the improvements your code will receive using TypeScript instead of JavaScript by building a simple console-based Library app. We won't worry about HTML, UI, or anything else. We will start by writing it in regular JavaScript and then transiting to TypeScript to see the difference.

Environment Setup

Let's set up our environment to write and run JavaScript files. If you already have a JavaScript environment set up, you can skip this section.

First, install Node.js on your computer. You can download it from nodejs.org and install it. Verify your installation is successful by opening a terminal or command prompt and run:
```
node -v
```

which will give you the version of Node you just installed. For e.g., I get something like:
```
(base) MacBook-Air-4:~ user$ node -v
v20.6.1
```

In the Terminal, create a new folder for your project and navigate into it. E.g.:
```
mkdir my-project
cd my-project
```

index.js

Open the *my-project* folder in a Code Editor of your choice. In this book, I am using VSCode. In VSCode, create a file named *index*.js and fill it with the following:

```
const library = [
    { title: "To Kill a Mockingbird", author: "Harper Lee",
availableCopies: 3 },
    { title: "1984", author: "George Orwell", availableCopies: 2 },
    { title: "Pride and Prejudice", author: "Jane Austen",
availableCopies: 4 },
    { title: "The Great Gatsby", author: "F. Scott Fitzgerald",
availableCopies: 2 },
]
```

```
EXPLORER              ···    JS index.js  ●
∨ MYPROJECT                  JS index.js > ...
  JS index.js               1   const library = [
                            2       { title: "To Kill a Mockingbird", author: "Harper Lee", availableCopies: 3 },
                            3       { title: "1984", author: "George Orwell", availableCopies: 2 },
                            4       { title: "Pride and Prejudice", author: "Jane Austen", availableCopies: 4 },
                            5       { title: "The Great Gatsby", author: "F. Scott Fitzgerald", availableCopies: 2 },
                            6   ]
```

(if you prefer to have the source codes for this book instead of manually copying and pasting, contact support@i-ducate.com)

We created a list of books represented in an array *library*. Each book has title, author, and available copies left for borrowing. We will keep track of the available copies for each book. When someone borrows a book, *availableCopies* will decrease by 1. When the book is returned, *availableCopies* will correspondingly increase by 1.

To keep track of loans, let's add in **bold**:

```
const library = [
    { title: "To Kill a Mockingbird", author: "Harper Lee",
availableCopies: 3 },
       ...
]

const loanQueue = []
```

We have a *loanQueue* initialized as an empty array.

Next, we add a little helper function called *addNewBook* which takes a *Book* object (that's just like the objects in our *library* array) and adds it to *library*. Add in **bold**:

```
const library = [
       ...
]

const loanQueue = []

function addNewBook(bookObj) {
    library.push(bookObj)
}
```

In *addNewBook*, we simply call *library.push* and pass in the book object.

Next, let's write another function *borrowBook* by adding in **bold**:

...

...

```
function addNewBook(bookObj) {
    library.push(bookObj)
}

function borrowBook(title) {
    const selectedBook = library.find(bookObj => bookObj.title === title)

    if(selectedBook.availableCopies <= 0){
        console.error(`${title} has no available copies`)
        return
    }
    selectedBook.availableCopies--

    const newLoan = { book: selectedBook, status: "borrowed" }
    loanQueue.push(newLoan)
    return newLoan
}
```

Code Explanation

```
function borrowBook(title) {
    const selectedBook = library.find(bookObj => bookObj.title === title)
```

We have a function *borrowBook* which takes a title. We then find *selectedBook* object by calling *library.find*. *find* is an array method where you provide a callback function.

.find will iterate over all the items in the array. If the callback function returns true at some point, *.find* will return the object it found and return it to *selectedBook*. In our case, we are looking for the *book* in *library* array with the *title* passed in. So if *bookObj.title* is equal to *title*, we have found our book object.

```
    if(selectedBook.availableCopies <= 0){
        console.error(`${title} has no available copies`)
        return
    }

    selectedBook.availableCopies--
```

We first check if *selectedBook* has *availableCopies* for us to borrow. If not, we log an error message and return. If *availableCopies* > 0, we go ahead and decrease *availableCopies* by 1.

```
    const newLoan = { book: selectedBook, status: "borrowed" }
```

11

Then we create a *newLoan* with *book* property that's going to be our *selectedBook* object, and *status* which we default to "borrowed".

```
loanQueue.push(newLoan)
return newLoan
```

We then push *newLoan* into *loanQueue*.

Loan id

Next, we add an *id* to the loan when we create them in *borrowBook*. Since we're not using a real database here, we create a global variable called *nextLoanId* that increments every time a new loan is placed to simulate real ids managed for us by a database.

Let's create a new variable *nextLoanId*, and set it equal to 1 to start:
```
...
const loanQueue = []
const nextLoanId = 1
...
```

In *borrowBook*, when creating our new Loan, we add an *id* property, and say, *nextLoanId++*:

```
function borrowBook(title) {
    const selectedBook = library.find(bookObj => bookObj.title === title)
        ...
    selectedBook.availableCopies--

    const newLoan = { id: nextLoanId++, book: selectedBook, status:
"borrowed" }
    loanQueue.push(newLoan)
    return newLoan
}
```

This will return the original *nextLoanId* before it gets incremented. That value will be set as the id for the current loan. After setting the id, it will increment *nextLoanId* for future use. For example, if *nextLoanId* is initially 1:
- the current loan gets an id of 1.
- *nextLoanId* is then incremented to 2.
- the next time *borrowBook* is called, the process repeats with 2 as the id, and *nextLoanId* becomes 3.

Now, I know there are bugs in here. We're going to fix that very soon.

returnBook

We next write a function called *returnBook* which takes a loan id as a parameter. *returnBook* will search our *loanQueue* array for the loan with that id, and mark its status as "returned" instead of "borrowed". Add in the codes:

```
function returnBook(loanId) {
    const loan = loanQueue.find(loan => loan.id === loanId)
    loan.status = "returned"
    loan.book.availableCopies++
    return loan
}
```

We use the *find* method as we did before. For each loan, we check if its id is equal to the *loanId* passed into this function. We then change the loan's status to "returned", increment the loaned book's *availableCopies* by 1, and return the updated loan.

Let's Test

Now, let's test a few things in our console Library app. We'll add a couple of new books with these codes:

```
...
function returnBook(loanId) {
        ...
}

addNewBook({ title: "One Hundred Years of Solitude", author: "Gabriel
García Márquez", availableCopies: 1 })
addNewBook({ title: "Brave New World", author: "Aldous Huxley",
availableCopies: 3 })
addNewBook({ title: "The Catcher in the Rye", author: "J.D. Salinger",
availableCopies: 2 })
```

Then, we place a loan for 'Brave New World'. And we also return the book. Add the codes:

```
borrowBook("Brave New World")
returnBook("1")
```

We test our *returnBook* function with the loan id of 1. To thoroughly check our progress, let's console log *library* and *loanQueue* to see if *addNewBook* is working correctly. So add:

```
console.log("Library:", library)
console.log("Loan queue:", loanQueue)
```

You might have noticed this code is riddled with some minor bugs. If you were to run through this program carelessly, one might think, "Well, this looks pretty good. Let's push this up to production." However, if you took the chance to pause and run this code, you'd know we'll encounter all kinds of little problems.

If we went back to the Terminal and run *index*.js with the command:

```
node index.js
```

First of all, we have "TypeError: assignment to a constant variable":

```
/Users/user/myproject/index.js:26
    const newLoan = { id: nextLoanId++, book: selectedBook, status: "borrowed" }
                         ^

TypeError: Assignment to constant variable.
    at borrowBook (/Users/user/myproject/index.js:26:37)
    at Object.<anonymous> (/Users/user/myproject/index.js:43:1)
    at Module._compile (node:internal/modules/cjs/loader:1241:14)
    at Module._extensions..js (node:internal/modules/cjs/loader:1295:10)
    at Module.load (node:internal/modules/cjs/loader:1091:32)
    at Module._load (node:internal/modules/cjs/loader:938:12)
    at Function.executeUserEntryPoint [as runMain] (node:internal/modules/run_main:83:12)
    at node:internal/main/run_main_module:23:47
```

This actually crashed our program.

If somehow this made it past testing and was pushed to production, our app would have crashed.

There's also a bug in the way I'm testing my *returnBook* function. I used a string "1" but it should be a number:

```
...
borrowBook("Brave New World")
returnBook("1")
...
function returnBook(loanId) {
    const loan = loanQueue.find(loan => loan.id === loanId)
    loan.status = "returned"
    loan.book.availableCopies++
    return loan
}
```

This would have probably crashed our program as well.

Now, before spending more time fixing these errors, it is the perfect opportunity to move this project over to TypeScript.

First, we'll see what errors TypeScript can identify without us making any changes to the code. Then, we'll dive deeper into TypeScript and explore how we can augment our code to teach TypeScript how things are supposed to work, enabling it to catch bugs it otherwise wouldn't detect.

So, before this bug-laden code causes any more anxiety, let's transition to TypeScript and see how we can address everything.

In case you got lost anywhere, here's the whole code of *index*.js:

```
const library = [
    { title: "To Kill a Mockingbird", author: "Harper Lee", availableCopies: 3 },
    { title: "1984", author: "George Orwell", availableCopies: 2 },
    { title: "Pride and Prejudice", author: "Jane Austen", availableCopies: 4 },
    { title: "The Great Gatsby", author: "F. Scott Fitzgerald", availableCopies:
2 },
]

const loanQueue = []
const nextLoanId = 1

function addNewBook(bookObj) {
    library.push(bookObj)
}

function borrowBook(title) {
    const selectedBook = library.find(bookObj => bookObj.title === title)

    if(selectedBook.availableCopies <= 0){
        console.error(`${title} has no available copies`)
        return
    }
    selectedBook.availableCopies--

    const newLoan = { id: nextLoanId++, book: selectedBook, status: "borrowed" }
    loanQueue.push(newLoan)
    return newLoan
}

function returnBook(loanId) {
    const loan = loanQueue.find(loan => loan.id === loanId)
    loan.status = "returned"
    loan.book.availableCopies++
    return loan
}
```

```
addNewBook({ title: "One Hundred Years of Solitude", author: "Gabriel García
Márquez", availableCopies: 1 })
addNewBook({ title: "Brave New World", author: "Aldous Huxley", availableCopies:
3 })
addNewBook({ title: "The Catcher in the Rye", author: "J.D. Salinger",
availableCopies: 2 })

borrowBook("Brave New World")
returnBook("1")

console.log("Library:", library)
console.log("Loan queue:", loanQueue)
```

Chapter 3: Transiting to TypeScript

Environment Setup

Before we proceed on, let's set up our development environment so we can start writing and running TypeScript files.

Because we have Node.js installed, you can use npm (Node Package Manager) to install TypeScript globally on your system (every folder can access the TypeScript compiler). In the Terminal, run:

```
npm install -g typescript
```

In your project folder, run the following command to create a *package*.json file:

```
npm init -y
```

Create a *tsconfig.json* file in your project folder by running:

```
tsc --init
```

This creates a default TypeScript configuration file. Now, let's start using TypeScript for this project and see what it offers us immediately out of the box.

Back in VSCode, **change our *index*.js JavaScript file to a *ts* file extension:**

If all is working, we should get a bunch of red squiggles:

```typescript
TS index.ts > ⬡ borrowBook
1   const library = [
2       { title: "To Kill a Mockingbird", author: "Harper Lee", availableCopies: 3 },
3       { title: "1984", author: "George Orwell", availableCopies: 2 },
4       { title: "Pride and Prejudice", author: "Jane Austen", availableCopies: 4 },
5       { title: "The Great Gatsby", author: "F. Scott Fitzgerald", availableCopies: 2 },
6   ]
7
8
9   const loanQueue = []
10  const nextLoanId = 1
11
12  function addNewBook(bookObj) {
13      library.push(bookObj)
14  }
15
16  function borrowBook(title) {
17      const selectedBook = library.find(bookObj => bookObj.title === title)
18
19      if(selectedBook.availableCopies <= 0){
20          console.error(`${title} has no available copies`)
21          return
22      }
23
24      selectedBook.availableCopies--
25
26      const newLoan = { id: nextLoanId++, book: selectedBook, status: "borrowed" }
27      loanQueue.push(newLoan)
```

Previously, JavaScript was pleased with our code. But TypeScript immediately warns us of potential errors.

Throughout this book, whenever you see these red squiggles, hover your cursor over them, read the IntelliSense popup, and see if there are any bugs you can fix right there.

For example, some are errors about variables implicitly having an *any* type:

```
{   const loanQueue: any[]
{
]   Variable 'loanQueue' implicitly has type 'any[]' in some locations where its type
    cannot be determined. ts(7034)

    View Problem (⌥F8)    Quick Fix... (⌘.)

const loanQueue = []
```

We will discuss *any* later in the book.

If you hover over *nextLoanId++*, it says you "Cannot assign to 'nextLoanId' because it is a constant":

```
                    const nextLoanId: 1

                    Cannot assign to 'nextLoanId' because it is a constant.
                    View Problem (⌥F8)   Quick Fix... (⌘.)
const newLoan = { id: nextLoanId++, book: selectedBook, status: "borrowed" }
```

This should be an obvious fix if you know the difference between *const* and *let*. Essentially, we can't assign a *const* new values later. So let's change this to a *let*:

```
...
const loanQueue = []
let nextLoanId = 1
...
```

By making this simple change, TypeScript is now satisfied when it comes to *nextLoanId*:

```
const loanQueue = []
let nextLoanId = 1

function addNewBook(bookObj) {
    library.push(bookObj)
}

function borrowBook(title) {
    const selectedBook = library.find(bookObj => bookObj.title === title)

    if(selectedBook.availableCopies <= 0){
        console.error(`${title} has no available copies`)
        return
    }

    selectedBook.availableCopies--

    const newLoan = { id: nextLoanId++, book: selectedBook, status: "borrowed" }
    loanQueue.push(newLoan)
    return newLoan
}
```

At first glance, using TypeScript seems intimidating because of the red squiggly lines and the additional code you must write to fix the errors.

However, a better way to think about this is TypeScript shows us the problems already existing in our code. TypeScript doesn't introduce new errors, but helps us find them immediately as we type our code instead of waiting for app crashes.

Over the next few chapters, we will fix these bugs, add new features to our app, and see where TypeScript is and isn't happy, all while using that to drive forward our knowledge of TypeScript.

Chapter 4: Defensive Coding

We can fix one more error before writing TypeScript-specific code here. And that's here:

```
function borrowBook(title) {
    const selectedBook = library.find(bookObj => bookObj.title === title)

    if(selectedBook.availableCopies <= 0){
        console.error(`${title} has no available copies`)
        return
  }
  ...
```

Hover your cursor over *selectedBook* here, and you'll see the pop up, "Object is possibly 'undefined'":

```
const selectedBook: {
    title: string;
    author: string;
    availableCopies: number;
} | undefined

functio
    con   Object is possibly 'undefined'. ts(2532)   bookObj.title === title)

          View Problem (⌥F8)   No quick fixes available
    if(selectedBook.availableCopies <= 0){
        console.error(`${title} has no available copies`)
        return

    }
```

This is an excellent example of how TypeScript can warn us about a potential problem.

Of course, assuming everything will work out perfectly when coding is lovely. But if you have, in the past, experienced code pushed to production that didn't account for edge cases, you know how important it is to account for and assume that problems will occur.

TypeScript helps us by forcing us to think of edge cases where problems can arise and address them in our code, before we have critical issues in production.

It is a more defensive way of coding. Granted, it takes work. You have to think about the edge cases in production. Imagining the unexpected ways users might use our app can be difficult.

Let's see how TypeScript helps us write code defensively. For example, with *selectedBook*:

```
    const selectedBook: {
        title: string;
        author: string;
        availableCopies: number;
    } | undefined
functio
    con                                           bookObj.title === title)
    Object is possibly 'undefined'. ts(2532)
    View Problem (⌥F8)   No quick fixes available
if(selectedBook.availableCopies <= 0){
    console.error(`${title} has no available copies`)
    return
}
```

When it tells us "Object is possibly 'undefined'", TypeScript is alerting us to a potential issue. When we try to find an item in our *library* array based on the book title, TypeScript can see it's possible *selectedBook* may come back as *undefined*.

```
function borrowBook(title) {
    const selectedBook = library.find(bookObj => bookObj.title === title)

    if(selectedBook.availableCopies <= 0){
    ...
```

If we're searching for a book that we misspelled or that doesn't exist in our *library*, then *selectedBook* will be undefined, and TypeScript says it would crash our program.

To satisfy TypeScript, we can code more defensively and say if there is no *selectedBook*, log *console.error()* with a message, "Book title does not exist in library." Add in **bold**:

```
function borrowBook(title) {
    const selectedBook = library.find(bookObj => bookObj.title === title)

    if (!selectedBook) {
        console.error(`${title} does not exist in library`)
        return
    }

    if(selectedBook.availableCopies <= 0){
        console.error(`${title} has no available copies`)
        return
    }
    ...
    ...
```

And *return* from this function.

By adding *return*, TypeScript is assured *if (selectedBook.availableCopies <= 0)* will never get reached if *selectedBook* is undefined.

I hope you see how we can identify potential bugs and fix a couple of them simply by including TypeScript in our project and using the *.ts* extension on our file. We still have some other errors, for example:

```
const loanQueue: any[]

Variable 'loanQueue' implicitly has type 'any[]' in some locations where its type
cannot be determined. ts(7034)

View Problem (⌥F8)    Quick Fix... (⌘.)
const loanQueue = []
let nextLoanId = 1
```

But we've reached the limit where TypeScript can't help us without defining specific TypeScript *types* in our program. Let's start learning some TypeScript specific types starting from the basics.

Chapter 5: Types

We're starting to see some of the benefits of using TypeScript. To really begin appreciating TypeScript, we have to learn some of the basics of TypeScript, and that is how to type a variable. For this chapter, let's create a new file *types*.ts.

In *types*.ts, when I'm writing vanilla JavaScript, I can say:

```
let favoriteColor = "blue"
```

Because TypeScript is a superset of JavaScript, any JavaScript code will be legitimate TypeScript code. Ironically, when you write a line of code like this, TypeScript is very smart and can infer the data type for the variable we just created.

If you hover your cursor over *favoriteColor*, you'll see a small pop-up that says "let *favoriteColor*: string":

```
x.ts >   let favoriteColor: string
let favoriteColor = "blue"
```

TypeScript has inferred that *favoriteColor* should be a string based on that we assign the string "blue" to it.

If I say *favoriteColor* equals a number, we get a red squiggly:

```
let favoriteColor = "blue"
favoriteColor = 5
```

Hover your cursor over *favoriteColor,* and it says "Type 'number' is not assignable to type 'string'.":

```
let favoriteColor: string

Type 'number' is not assignable to type 'string'.

View Problem (⌥F8)    No quick fixes available
favoriteColor = 5
```

In other words, TypeScript is not happy we're trying to reassign a number value to a string variable.

Note: sometimes people talk about JavaScript's dynamic typing nature, for example the operation:

```
let favoriteColor = "blue"
favoriteColor = 5
```

is not a problem at all. They talk about JavaScript's flexibility. But in the real world, there is no reason why this would be a benefit. i.e. to reassign a string variable to something of a completely different data type. It is bad structuring of code. So TypeScript forces us to organize our code better. Let's get back to manual typing.

Although TypeScript correctly derived that *favoriteColor* is a string type, I can manually assign a type by typing a colon ':' immediately after my variable name, and then typing out the data type I want this to be:

```
let favoriteColor: string = "blue"
```

This is one of the instances where the TypeScript syntax is different from JavaScript syntax. This would not be correct syntax in vanilla JavaScript. But it is something you see throughout TypeScript.

We've already used the primitive data type of string. In TypeScript, the other two primitive data types we'll use are *number* and *boolean*. For example:

```
let favoriteColor: string = "blue"
let availableBooks: number = 250;
let isOpenOnSundays: boolean = true;
```

There's a little bit more syntax we're going to learn later when it comes to manually providing some types.

Add Type to *Loan id*

Back in *index*.ts, let's apply what we've learned to our Library app. Let's tell TypeScript what data type should be used for the *loanId* parameter in our *returnBook* function:

Index.ts

```
function returnBook(loanId) {
    const loan = loanQueue.find(loan => loan.id === loanId)
    loan.status = "returned"
    loan.book.availableCopies++
    return loan
}
```

We add in **bold**:

```
function returnBook(loanId: number) {
      ...
}
```

Once we add that, notice a new warning in the call to *returnBook("1")*:

```
                    Argument of type 'string' is not assignable to parameter of type 'number'.
borrowBook(  View Problem (⌥F8)   No quick fixes available
returnBook("1")
```

Because we've specified that the *loanId* parameter to *returnBook* is *number* type, TypeScript now knows we're using this function incorrectly.

We're passing in a string "1" where it shouldn't be. It says "Argument of type 'string' is not assignable to a parameter of type 'number'":.

Let's go ahead and make that a number:

```
returnBook(1)
```

The warning will go away. Our program has other potential issues. But before we resolve them, understand that because we're using TypeScript, we no longer crash with type errors.

At this point, our app would benefit from us writing custom types. Let's learn that in the next chapter.

Chapter 6: Defining Custom Types

We've discussed a few primitive types, such as string, number, and boolean, but in TypeScript, we can also create our own custom types.

We can create new types using the 'type' keyword. 'type' exists only in TypeScript. By convention, the name that we give our type starts with a capital letter. For example, let's create a new file *custom_types*.ts, and add:

```
type Instrument = string
let primaryInstrument: Instrument = "guitar"
```

By doing this, we now could use 'Instrument' as a new type to the `primaryInstrument` variable.

'type' comes in handy for creating custom types around objects. For example, I have this *vehicle* object with three properties: *model*, *year*, and *isElectric*.

```
let vehicle = {
    model: "Civic",
    year: 2021,
    isElectric: false
}
```

A common thing with objects is you have multiples of the same kind of object. So let's say we have *vehicle2*, which looks similar:

```
let vehicle2 = {
    model: "Model 3",
    year: 2023,
    iselectric: true
}
```

As it stands, there's no problem with this code. However, you might have noticed I used a lowercase 'e' in `iselectric` property for *vehicle2*.

One benefit of TypeScript is it forces consistentency. Although this may not now cause a bug, it will down the road. What we can do is create a custom type of an object to define the object with the exact property (case-sensitive) names.

We create a custom type using the *type* keyword and set it to an object with the properties we want. For e.g.:

29

```
type Vehicle = {
    model: string
    year: number
    isElectric: boolean
}
```

For example, we have *model*, and we give it the type *string*.

Note: for custom object types, you can use commas or semicolons between properties, you can also leave them out. In our case, we left them out. Just stay consistent in your code.

By defining *Vehicle* as a custom type, we added an extra degree of type safety. We can now define *vehicle1* and *vehicle2* like:

```
type Vehicle = {
    model: string
    year: number
    isElectric: boolean
}

let vehicle1: Vehicle = {
    model: "Civic",
    year: 2021,
    isElectric: false
}

let vehicle2: Vehicle = {
    model: "Model 3",
    year: 2023,
    iselectric: true
}
```

And the editor highlights an error now with *iselectric: true* for *vehicle2*. So let's correct this:

```
let vehicle2: Vehicle = {
    model: "Model 3",
    year: 2023,
    isElectric: true
}
```

This satisfies TypeScript. Let's apply this in our Library app.

Adding a *Book* Type

Let's standardize in our Library app what properties our book objects should have. In *index*.ts, we create a *Book* object type with properties *title*, *author* and *availableCopies*:

```
type Book = {
    title: string
    author: string
    availableCopies: number
}

const library = [
    ...
    ]
...
```

Before we carry on, notice in *addNewBook*, we have a warning:

```
(parameter) bookObj: any

Parameter 'bookObj' implicitly has an 'any' type.

View Problem (⌥F8)    Quick Fix... (⌘.)

function addNewBook(bookObj) {
    library.push(bookObj)
}
```

TypeScript warns that *bookObj* implicitly has an *any* type. We will dig into what *any* means later. But to resolve this now, we instruct *addNewBook* that *bookObj* is supposed to be of type *Book* by adding in **bold**:

```
function addNewBook(bookObj: Book) {
    library.push(bookObj)
}
```

With this, TypeScript should no longer warn us that *bookObject* is implicitly an *any* type. In fact if you hover your mouse over *bookObject*:

```
(parameter) bookObj: Book
function addNewBook(bookObj: Book) {
    library.push(bookObj)
}
```

it specifically tells you it's a parameter of type *Book*.

Currently, we call *addNewBook* to add books:

31

```
addNewBook({ title: "One Hundred Years of Solitude", author: "Gabriel
García Márquez", availableCopies: 1 })
addNewBook({ title: "Brave New World", author: "Aldous Huxley",
availableCopies: 3 })
addNewBook({ title: "The Catcher in the Rye", author: "J.D. Salinger",
availableCopies: 2 })
```

The code doesn't give us any problems because the properties *title*, *author*, and *availableCopies* in the object fit what is in *Book* type.

However, if we change the property from *title* to *name* for example:

```
(property) name: string

Argument of type '{ name: string; author: string; availableCopies: number; }' is not
assignable to parameter of type 'Book'.
    Object literal may only specify known properties, and 'name' does not exist in type
'Book'. ts(2345)

View Problem (⌥F8)    No quick fixes available
addNewBook({ name: "One Hundred Years of Solitude", author: "Gabriel García Márquez", availableCopies: 1 })
```

We get an error specifically "'name' does not exist in type 'Book'". So you see how TypeScript can identify such errors and prevent unnecessary crashes in production. Make sure to change *name* back to *title*.

Currently, we have an array *library* of *Book* items we initialized in the beginning:

```
const library = [
    { title: "To Kill a Mockingbird", author: "Harper Lee",
availableCopies: 3 },
    { title: "1984", author: "George Orwell", availableCopies: 2 },
    { title: "Pride and Prejudice", author: "Jane Austen",
availableCopies: 4 },
    { title: "The Great Gatsby", author: "F. Scott Fitzgerald",
availableCopies: 2 },
]
```

The same error could exist where we supply wrong or misspelled properties. That might cause bugs to crash our app down the road. But by defining *Book* type, we could defend against this problem.

Before we move on, let's fix our *borrowBook* function. If we hover over *title*:

```
(parameter) title: any

Parameter 'title' implicitly has an 'any' type.

View Problem (⌥F8)   Quick Fix... (⌘.)
function borrowBook(title) {
    const selectedBook = library.find(bookObj => bookObj.title === ti
```

We get the warning that *title* implicitly has an *any* type. Let's type that as a string and get rid of that warning:

```
function borrowBook(title: string) {
```

It looks like the issues we have left, have to do with *loanQueue*:

```
const loanQueue = []
let nextLoanId = 1
```

So let's go ahead and tackle this issue next.

Chapter 7: Nested Object Types

In *custom_types.ts*, suppose we want to expand our *Vehicle* object and include an *engine* property. An engine wouldn't simply be represented by a string, but instead by a nested object. For example:

```
type Vehicle = {
    model: string
    year: number
    isElectric: boolean
    engine: {
        type: string
        horsepower: number
        fuelType: string
    }
}
```

The nested object *engine*, contains *type*, *horsepower*, and *fuelType*. When we change the definition for *Vehicle* to say it must include an engine, a red squiggly will appear in a *Vehicle* object if it does not contain an *engine*:

```
let vehicle1: Vehicle

Property 'engine' is missing in type '{ model: string; year: number; isElectric:
false; }' but required in type 'Vehicle'. ts(2741)

index.ts(17, 5): 'engine' is declared here.

View Problem (⌥F8)    No quick fixes available
let vehicle1: Vehicle = {
    model: "Civic",
    year: 2021,
    isElectric: false
}
```

To rectify this, we have to put an *engine* in the object:

```
let vehicle1: Vehicle = {
    model: "Civic",
    year: 2021,
    isElectric: false,
    engine: {
        type: "Inline-4",
        horsepower: 158,
        fuelType: "Gasoline"
    }
}
```

As soon as we add an *engine*, it satisfies the definition for *Vehicle* type, and TypeScript stops complaining. Removing any one of these properties is going to make TypeScript complain because it won't perfectly match the *Vehicle* type.

Another common way to structure nested objects is to create a separate type for *engine* alone. E.g.:

```
type Engine = {
    type: string
    horsepower: number
    fuelType: string
}

type Vehicle = {
    model: string
    year: number
    isElectric: boolean
    engine: Engine
}
```

Either way is fine. If you think you will use *Engine* type elsewhere as a standalone type, it makes sense to separate it into its own *Engine* type. Or if you know *Engine* will only exist as an object in the context of a *Vehicle* object, just leave it nested inside of *Vehicle*.

In the next chapter, we will talk about how we can make properties optional.

Chapter 8: Optional Properties

If you are worried about TypeScript's rigidity in object types, you can make properties optional. However, this comes with the trade-off of reduced type safety, which we will discuss later.

When defining a custom type, we can put a question mark after the property name that's going to be optional. For example, in *custom_types*.ts, we mark *Engine* as optional:

```
type Vehicle = {
    model: string
    year: number
    isElectric: boolean
    engine?: Engine
}
```

And this will now be allowed:

```
let vehicle2: Vehicle = {
    model: "Model 3",
    year: 2023,
    isElectric: true
}
```

Although this offers flexibility, however, it does reduce type safety. For example, we have a function *displayVehicleInfo* which takes a *Vehicle* as a parameter:

```
function displayVehicleInfo(vehicle: Vehicle) {
    console.log(`${vehicle.model} has a ${vehicle.engine.type} engine.`)
}
```

But we will get an error that *vehicle.engine* is possibly 'undefined':

```
                            (property) engine?: Engine | undefined

                            Object is possibly 'undefined'. ts(2532

function displayVehicleInfo(vehicle: Vehic  View Problem (⌥F8)   No quick fixes available
    console.log(`${vehicle.model} has a ${vehicle.engine.type} engine.`)
}
```

We can technically get rid of this error by using optional chaining on *engine*:

```
function displayVehicleInfo(vehicle: Vehicle) {
    console.log(`${vehicle.model} has a ${vehicle.engine?.type} engine.`)
}
```

We can run our app with a call to *displayVehicleInfo(vehicle2)*. Our entire file will look something like:

```typescript
type Engine = {
    type: string
    horsepower: number
    fuelType: string
}

type Vehicle = {
    model: string
    year: number
    isElectric: boolean
    engine?: Engine
}

let vehicle2: Vehicle = {
    model: "Model 3",
    year: 2023,
    isElectric: true
}

function displayVehicleInfo(vehicle: Vehicle) {
    console.log(`${vehicle.model} has a ${vehicle.engine?.type} engine.`)
}

displayVehicleInfo(vehicle2)
```

Running our TypeScript file

Let's run our app. To run our TypeScript file, we first need to compile *index*.ts into JavaScript.

Compile our *custom_types*.ts by running *tsc custom_types*.ts. And after compilation, it will generate an *custom_types*.js file. Now you can run the compiled JavaScript using Node.js:

```
node custom_types.js
```

And we get a "Model 3 has a undefined engine" message:

```
Model 3 has a undefined engine.
```

Though showing 'undefined' is not a program crashing type error, it is still not a great experience.

So just note that adding an optional property is legitimate and common to do in TypeScript. Just that when we increase flexibility through using optionals, you reduce your type safety by a bit.

Let's move on and apply what we've learned to our Library app.

In case you got lost anywhere, here's the full code for *custom_types*.ts:

```typescript
type Instrument = string
let primaryInstrument: Instrument = "guitar"

type Engine = {
    type: string
    horsepower: number
    fuelType: string
}

type Vehicle = {
    model: string
    year: number
    isElectric: boolean
    engine?: Engine
}

let vehicle1: Vehicle = {
    model: "Civic",
    year: 2021,
    isElectric: false,
    engine: {
        type: "Inline-4",
        horsepower: 158,
        fuelType: "Gasoline"
    }
}

let vehicle2: Vehicle = {
    model: "Model 3",
    year: 2023,
    isElectric: true
}

function displayVehicleInfo(vehicle: Vehicle) {
    console.log(`${vehicle.model} has a ${vehicle.engine?.type} engine.`)
}

displayVehicleInfo(vehicle2)
```

Chapter 9: Adding a *Loan* Type

In *index*.ts, let's now create a *Loan* type with an *id*, *book*, and *status*:

```
type Book = {
      ...
}

type Loan = {
    id: number
    book: Book
    status: string
}
```

Now you might notice there's a warning on *loanQueue*:

```
const loanQueue: any[]

Variable 'loanQueue' implicitly has type 'any[]' in some locations where its type
cannot be determined. ts(7034)

View Problem (⌥F8)   Quick Fix... (⌘.)
const loanQueue = []
let nextLoanId = 1
```

And even if you did this:
```
const loanQueue: Loan = []
```

It doesn't fix the warning TypeScript is giving us. That's because the *loanQueue* is an array, it's not a single object. To specify that it's an array, we put a set of square brackets '[]' right after the *Loan* type:

```
const loanQueue: Loan[] = []
```

So TypeScript knows that *loanQueue* is an array of *Loan* objects and no longer complains about *loanQueue*. Now, we only have one more TypeScript warning:

```
function returnBook(loanId: number) {
    const loan = loanQueue.find(loan => loan.id === loanId)
    loan.status = "returned"
    loan.book.availableCopies++
    return loan
}
```

It says "Object is possibly 'undefined'":

41

```
const loan: Loan | undefined
Object is possibly 'undefined'. ts(2532)
View Problem (⌥F8)   No quick fixes available        === loanId)
loan.status = "returned"
loan.book.availableCopies++
return loan
```

This should look familiar as it is the same warning we got when we wrote:
selectedBook.availableCopies. It was telling us that *selectedBook* is possibly undefined:

```
function borrowBook(title: string) {
    const selectedBook = library.find(bookObj => bookObj.title === title)

    if (!selectedBook) {
       console.error(`${title} does not exist in library`)
       return
     }

    if(selectedBook.availableCopies <= 0){
        console.error(`${title} has no available copies`)
        return
    }
    ...
```

So we do something similar in *returnBook*. Add in **bold**:

```
function returnBook(loanId: number) {
    const loan = loanQueue.find(loan => loan.id === loanId)
    if (!loan) {
        console.error(`${loanId} was not found in the loan queue`);
        return;
    }
    loan.status = "returned"
    loan.book.availableCopies++
    return loan
}
```

If there is no loan, we console error, "*loanId* was not found in loan queue" and we return.
If we want however, we could also throw an error by changing in **bold**:

```
function returnBook(loanId: number) {
    const loan = loanQueue.find(loan => loan.id === loanId)
    if (!loan) {
        console.error(`${loanId} was not found in the loan queue`);
        throw new Error()
    }
    ...
```

If we throw an error, it halts the execution of this function and TypeScript is satisfied that *loan.status* is never going to get reached if loan is non-existent.

All the TypeScript warnings in our app should be gone now. The lack of TypeScript warnings doesn't mean that our program will function exactly as we expect, nor does it mean we've handled every edge case. But it does mean we have greater confidence that our app will work as expected.

My code currently looks something like:

…

…

```
addNewBook({ title: "Brave New World", author: "Aldous Huxley", availableCopies: 3 })

borrowBook("Brave New World")
returnBook(1)

console.log("Library:", library)
console.log("Loan queue:", loanQueue)
```

If we compile our *index.ts* now by running *tsc index.ts*, we might get these compilation errors:

```
(base) MacBook-Air-4:my-project user$ tsc index.ts
index.ts:28:36 - error TS2550: Property 'find' does not exist on type '{ title: string; author
: string; availableCopies: number; }[]'. Do you need to change your target library? Try changi
ng the 'lib' compiler option to 'es2015' or later.
```

```
28     const selectedBook = library.find(bookObj => bookObj.title === title)
                                    ~~~~
```

```
index.ts:  :   - error TS2550: Property 'find' does not exist on type 'Loan[]'. Do you need to
 change your target library? Try changing the 'lib' compiler option to 'es2015' or later.
```

```
47     const loan = loanQueue.find(loan => loan.id === loanId)
                              ~~~~
```

```
Found 2 errors in the same file, starting at: index.ts:28
```

[show

Thus, we need to specify the following compilation configurations in *tsconfig.*json:

…

```
    "target": "es6",
    "lib": ["es6", "dom", "es2016"],
```

…

These allow us to use the newer JavaScript features in our TypeScript code like *find()*.

Note: Don't be intimidated by all these settings in *tsconfig.json*. You don't have to learn all of them, and nobody knows all of them. I don't know all of them either.

Because we have updated options defined in *tsconfig.*json, we run the command:

```
tsc --project ./tsconfig.json
```

to run the TypeScript compiler with the updated configurations in *tsconfig*.json.

And after you compile *index*.ts, it will generate an *index*.js file. Now you can run the compiled JavaScript using Node.js:

```
node index.js
```

And we get the following:

```
(base) MacBook-Air-4:myproject user$ tsc --project ./tsconfig.json
(base) MacBook-Air-4:myproject user$ node index.js
Library: [
  {
    title: 'To Kill a Mockingbird',
    author: 'Harper Lee',
    availableCopies: 3
  },
  { title: '1984', author: 'George Orwell', availableCopies: 2 },
  {
    title: 'Pride and Prejudice',
    author: 'Jane Austen',
    availableCopies: 4
  },
  {
    title: 'The Great Gatsby',
    author: 'F. Scott Fitzgerald',
    availableCopies: 2
  },
  {
    title: 'Brave New World',
    author: 'Aldous Huxley',
    availableCopies: 3
  }
]
Loan queue: [
  {
    id: 1,
    book: {
      title: 'Brave New World',
      author: 'Aldous Huxley',
      availableCopies: 3
    },
    status: 'returned'
  }
]
```

Everything looks the way we expect. We will build some more features in our Library app to touch on a few more topics in TypeScript.

Chapter 10: Unions

Let's say in our application, we want a *vehicleType* variable to hold the values either 'motorcycle', 'car', or 'truck'. Only these values are allowed. We don't want a *vehicleType* like 'aeroplane' or something gibberish that doesn't make sense to our application.

In this scenario, we can use a concept called unions to teach TypeScript that *vehicleType* should only be allowed to be one of a certain number of strings.

In *custom_types*.ts, let's create a new type called *VehicleType* like the below:

```
type VehicleType = "motorcycle" | "car" | "truck";

let vehicleType: VehicleType = "car";
```

We can make a union using the pipe character '|'. We say that type `VehicleType` is either going to be the string literal *motorcycle* or the string literal *car* or the string literal *truck*. After defining what a `VehicleType` type is allowed to be, we can tell `vehicleType` variable to conform to `VehicleType` type.

If we change this to some gibberish, TypeScript would give a warning:

```
type VehicleType = "motorcycle" | "car" | "truck";

let vehicleType: VehicleType = "abc";
```

We can also use Unions nested inside in another type. In our *Vehicle* type, we can add a *vehicleType* property which has to be one of these three string literals:

```
type Vehicle = {
    model: string
    year: number
    isElectric: boolean
    engine?: Engine
    vehicleType: "motorcycle" | "car" | "truck"
}
```

After making this change, we also add *vehicleType* to *vehicle1* and *vehicle2*:

45

```
let vehicle1: Vehicle = {
    model: "Civic",
    year: 2021,
    isElectric: false,
    engine: {
        type: "Inline-4",
        horsepower: 158,
        fuelType: "Gasoline"
    },
    vehicleType: 'car'
}

let vehicle2: Vehicle = {
    model: "Model 3",
    year: 2023,
    isElectric: true,
    vehicleType: 'car'
}
```

Update Loan Status to use Unions

We can add extra type safety to our loans by teaching TypeScript that a loan status can't be just any string. It has to be the string 'borrowed', or 'returned'.

In *index*.ts, let's update our loan type:

```
type Loan = {
    id: number
    book: Book
    status: "borrowed" | "returned"
}
```

Having made this change, we see a new TypeScript warning:

```
if(selectedBook    Argument of type '{ id: number; book: { title: string; author:
    console.err    string; availableCopies: number; }; status: string; }' is not
    return         assignable to parameter of type 'Loan'.
}                     Types of property 'status' are incompatible.
selectedBook.av          Type 'string' is not assignable to type '"borrowed" |
                   "returned"'. ts(2345)
const newLoan =  View Problem (⌥F8)   No quick fixes available
loanQueue.push(newLoan)
return newLoan
```

It has to do with this line:

46

```
...
    const newLoan = { id: nextLoanId++, book: selectedBook, status:
"borrowed" }
    loanQueue.push(newLoan)
...
```

This is because previously, we have specified that *loanQueue* is an array of *Loan* objects:
```
const loanQueue: Loan[] = []
```

We can fix this error by telling TypeScript specifically this is an *Loan* type:
```
const newLoan: Loan = { id: nextLoanId++, book: selectedBook, status:
"borrowed" }
```

Now, if I were to change this:
```
const newLoan: Loan = { id: nextLoanId++, book: selectedBook, status: "blah" }
loanQueue.push(newLoan)
return newLoan
```

TypeScript will complain again because it knows *status* has to be either *borrowed* or *returned*. The same would happen if we change in *returnBook*:
```
function returnBook(loanId: number) {
    const loan = loanQueue.find(loan =
    if (!loan) {
        console.error(`${loanId} was n
        return;
    }
    loan.status = "blah"
    loan.book.availableCopies++
    return loan
}
```

Chapter 11: Add *id* to Book

Currently we don't have *id* in our *Book* type. So let's add it in *index*.ts:

```
type Book = {
    id: number
    title: string
    author: string
    availableCopies: number
}
```

We also haven't specified that *library* is an array of *Book* objects. So let's go ahead and type it as an array of *Book*(s):

```
const library: Book[] = [
    { title: "To Kill a Mockingbird", author: "Harper Lee"… },
        …
]
```

TypeScript will warn us there's an *id* property missing in these objects. And that's a good warning. So let's add *id*:

```
const library: Book[] = [
    { id:1, title: "To Kill a Mockingbird", author: "Harper Lee", … },
    { id:2, title: "1984", author: "George Orwell", … },
    { id:3, title: "Pride and Prejudice", author: "Jane Austen", … },
    { id:4, title: "The Great Gatsby", author: "F. Scott Fitzgerald" … },
]
```

We also get an error with *addNewBook*, because of the missing *id*:

```
addNewBook({ title: "Brave New World", author: "Aldous Huxley", availableCopies: 3 })
```

So let's manually add ids too:

```
addNewBook({ id:5, title: "Brave New World", author: "Aldous Huxley"… })
```

Manually adding ids is just a temporary fix. We will implement a more permanent solution later.

Hopefully, you see how TypeScript doesn't make your job harder as a developer, but improves your ability to add new features and debug your code in the process. When we made an update to the *Book* type, TypeScript immediately showed where the problems with that change would happen.

Next, we'll move on to a concept called type narrowing.

Chapter 12: Type Narrowing

To understand type narrowing, in *index*.ts, let's create a new function *getBookDetail* which takes a single parameter *identifier*. But we allow *identifier* to be either the string title of a book eg. "Brave New World" or it could be an id eg. '5'. So we have:

```
function getBookDetail(identifier: string | number) {
  // Function body would go here
}
```

Here, we can also use unions in parameter types.

Next, let's use the identifier (whether it's a string or a number), and use *library.find* to find a *Book* from *library* and return that book. Add in the code:

```
function getBookDetail(identifier: string | number) {
    if (typeof identifier === "string") {
        return library.find(book => book.title === identifier)
    }
}
```

In JavaScript, we can determine what kind of data type *identifier* has by using the *typeof* keyword. If the *typeof identifier* is a string, we assume it's the title of the book, and return what comes back from *library.find*. For every book we're looking through, if *book.title* is equal to *identifier*, it will find the correct book and return it.

To make the code more robust, we lowercase both so if a user puts in the wrong capitalization for the book title, it can still find the correct book. Add in **bold**:

```
function getBookDetail(identifier: string | number) {
    if (typeof identifier === "string") {
        return library.find(book =>
            book.title.toLowerCase() === identifier.toLowerCase())
    }
}
```

Next we use an *else* when the type of *identifier* is a *number*:

```
function getBookDetail(identifier: string | number) {
    if (typeof identifier === "string") {
        return library.find(book =>
            book.title.toLowerCase() === identifier.toLowerCase())
    } else {
        return library.find(book => book.id === identifier)
    }
}
```

We do a similar check but instead of *title*, we check by *id*. Note: we don't need *toLowerCase* here because *id* is a number.

Now, if you hover your cursor over *identifier* in the *else* clause, it will tell you that *identifier* is *number* type:

```typescript
function getBookDetail(identifier: string | number) {
    if (typeof identifier === "string") {
        return library.find(book =>
            book.title.toLowerCase() === identifier.toLowerCase())
    } else {                          (parameter) identifier: number
        return library.find(book => book.id === identifier)
    }
}
```

This is an example of type narrowing, where TypeScript narrows down the type and handles each use case. Later, we will see another example where type narrowing is important.

Chapter 13: Function Return Types

In *index*.ts, we have a function *borrowBook* which returns the *newLoan* we added to *loanQueue*:

```
function borrowBook(title: string) {
    ...
    ...
    const newLoan: Loan = { id: nextLoanId++, book: selectedBook, ... }
    loanQueue.push(newLoan)
    return newLoan
}
```

When you hover your cursor over the name of the function *borrowBook*:

```
    function borrowBook(title: string): Loan | undefined
function borrowBook(title: string) {
    const selectedBook = library.find(bookObj => bookObj.title === title)
```

We see in the popup its return type is "Loan | undefined". TypeScript was able to infer we either return *newLoan* which is a *Loan* type, or it returns *undefined* caused by the below:

```
...
    if (!selectedBook) {
        console.error(`${title} does not exist in library`)
        return
    }

    if(selectedBook.availableCopies <= 0){
        console.error(`${title} has no available copies`)
        return
    }
...
```

But in many instances, it is helpful to explicitly type what should be returned from your function. For example, we can add in **bold**:

```
function borrowBook(title: string): Loan {...
```

to teach TypeScript *borrowBook* should always return a *Loan* object. This however creates an issue with the below *return*:

```
function borrowBook(title: string): Loan {
    const selectedBook = library.find(bookObj => bookObj.tit

    if (!selectedBook) {
        console.error(`${title} does not exist in library`)
        return
    }

    if(selectedBook.availableCopies <= 0){
        console.error(`${title} has no available copies`)
        return
    }
```

We get the error:

```
if (    Type 'undefined' is not assignable to type 'Loan'.

        View Problem (⌥F8)    No quick fixes available

        return
}
```

To resolve it, I can explicitly state the return type as:

```
function borrowBook(title: string): Loan | undefined {
```

But why is it helpful to explicitly state a function's return type? One major reason is that it helps when we refactor our code.

If some other developer were to find *borrowBook* and say, I don't know why it's returning "*Loan | undefined*", it should be returning *loanQueue* instead:

```
    const newLoan: Loan = { id:
    loanQueue.push(newLoan)
    return loanQueue
}
```

If they try to do that, they get a warning from TypeScript.

And if we don't include this explicit return type declaration, then TypeScript has no problem with us changing the return value of this function. For example:

```
function borrowBook(title: string) {
    const selectedBook = library.find(bookObj => bookObj.title === title)

    if (!selectedBook) {...
    }

    if(selectedBook.availableCopies <= 0){...
    }

    selectedBook.availableCopies--

    const newLoan: Loan = { id: nextLoanId++, book: selectedBook, status:
    loanQueue.push(newLoan)
    return loanQueue
}
```

And this would definitely cause problems. So this is a chance to be more explicit and specify we want to return "*Loan | undefined*":

```
function borrowBook(title: string): Loan | undefined {...
```

And if we really want to change the return of this function to *return loanQueue*, we have to explicitly change the return type:

```
function borrowBook(title: string): Loan[] | undefined {
    ...
    ...
    const newLoan: Loan = { id: nextLoanId++, book: selectedBook, ... }
    loanQueue.push(newLoan)
    return loanQueue
}
```

By specifying the return types of functions, other developers know what a function is explicitly returning.

Let's change it back to return *Loan | undefined* for now:

```
function borrowBook(title: string): Loan | undefined {
    ...
    ...
    const newLoan: Loan = { id: nextLoanId++, book: selectedBook, ... }
    loanQueue.push(newLoan)
    return newLoan
}
```

Add return type to *getBookDetail*

To affirm our understanding of types. Let's add a return *Book* type to the *getBookDetail* function:

```
function getBookDetail(identifier: string | number): Book {...
```

Like before, we get these TypeScript warnings:

```
function getBookDetail(identifier: string | number): Book {
    if (typeof identifier === "string") {
        return library.find(book =>
            book.title.toLowerCase() === identifier.toLowerCase())
    } else {
        return library.find(book => book.id === identifier)
    }
}
```

It tells us that type 'Book | undefined' is not assignable to type 'Book'.

```
            Type 'Book | undefined' is not assignable to type 'Book'.
                Type 'undefined' is not assignable to type 'Book'. ts(2322)
function
    if (  View Problem (⌥F8)    No quick fixes available
        return library.find(book =>
            book.title.toLowerCase() === identifier.toLowerCase())
    } else {
        return library.find(book => book.id === identifier)
    }
}
```

This is because *library.find* potentially returns an undefined value if it's not able to find the book you specified. TypeScript was smart enough to read through the code and know we potentially return *undefined* here. So it inferred the return type as "Book | undefined".

So let's change the return type of *getBookDetail* to:

```
function getBookDetail(identifier: string | number): Book | undefined {...
```

Like we saw before, this doesn't change how the function works. But it does help other developers in the future know when reading this code to either make sure we continue to return a *Book* or *undefined*.

Void Return Type

There's another return type that's more subtle. If you hover your mouse over *addNewBook*, you'll see the inferred return type is *void*:

```
function addNewBook(bookObj: Book): void
function addNewBook(bookObj: Book) {
    library.push(bookObj)
}
```

addNewBook modifies *library* by pushing new objects to it, but it doesn't return anything. So, we can state that this function doesn't return anything by explicitly typing this as returning *void*:

```
function addNewBook(bookObj: Book): void {
    library.push(bookObj)
}
```

This doesn't change how *addNewBook* operates. If you try to get the return value from calling *addNewBook*, you would get the value *undefined*.

But it helps us, or other developers in the future reviewing through this code know this wouldn't return anything. It's just performing an operation and not returning anything. So, *void* is pretty straightforward.

Now to make our app complete, we can also state the return type of `returnBook`:

```
function returnBook(loanId: number): Loan {
    const loan = loanQueue.find(loan => loan.id === loanId)
    if (!loan) {
        console.error(`${loanId} was not found in the loan queue`);
        //return;
        throw new Error()
    }
    loan.status = "returned"
    loan.book.availableCopies++
    return loan
}
```

And if there isn't a loan (*!loan*), we *throw new Error()* instead of returning *undefined*.

As a general guide, for any function that doesn't yet have a return type, we can just hover over it, see what the inferred type is, and explicitly state the return type.

Chapter 14: *Any* Type

Let's talk about a notorious type in TypeScript called *Any*. The easiest way to think about *Any* is to know that if you type something with *Any*, you're essentially turning off TypeScript checking for that variable.

So if I have a variable *temperature*, and set it to 72:

```
    let temperature: number
let temperature = 72
```

TypeScript is able to infer this should be of type number.

It gives me warnings if I try to re-assign it to a string or if I try to run an operation on it like *.slice()*, which only works for strings:

```
let temperature = 72
temperature = "warm"
temperature.slice(0, 2)
```

These warnings as we've seen until now, are useful to us. But if I manually type this as an *any* type. The warnings go away:

```
let temperature: any = 72
temperature = "warm"
temperature.slice(0, 2)
```

When we use *any*, we essentially say we know better than TypeScript how this variable should be typed and don't want TypeScript to help (and this is probably not a good idea). So when should we use *any*?

In short, we shouldn't. It can be tempting when you're looking at your code that has a bunch of TypeScript errors, type things as *any* so warnings go away, and continue on with coding. But in that case, why choose TypeScript in the first place?

One legitimate use case would be if you're transitioning your code base from JavaScript to TypeScript, and you don't have the time now to write all of the complex types and update all of your code to satisfy the TypeScript warnings, and you need a temporary way to get around TypeScript. Note the word **'temporary'**.

But be warned, as soon as you start adding *any* to your codebase, and the warnings go away, it will be difficult to go back and force yourself to bring those warnings back by removing the *any* types.

Any more on *any* (no pun intended) is outside the scope of this book. So if there's one thing to take away from this short chapter, just don't use *any*.

If you do have a scenario where there's a variable you legitimately don't know the type of, there's another TypeScript specific type much better suited for that scenario. It's called *Unknown* but is outside the scope of this book.

Chapter 15: Automatically Assign ids to Library Books

Let's do a simple refactoring of our code and see how TypeScript helps us. Currently, when we're creating the *library* array, we manually assign ids:

```
const library: Book[] = [
    { id:1, title: "To Kill a Mockingbird", author: "Harper Lee", … },
    { id:2, title: "1984", author: "George Orwell", availableCopies: 2 },
    { id:3, title: "Pride and Prejudice", author: "Jane Austen", … },
    { id:4, title: "The Great Gatsby", author: "F. Scott Fitzgerald"… },
]
```

The same with adding new Books:

```
addNewBook({ id:5, title: "Brave New World", author: "Aldous Huxley"… })
```

Let's use the same trick we're using with *nextLoanId*, where when creating a loan, we create an object and use *nextLoanId++*:

```
const loanQueue: Loan[] = []
let nextLoanId = 1
…

function borrowBook(title: string): Loan | undefined {
    const selectedBook = library.find(bookObj => bookObj.title === title)
    …
    const newLoan: Loan = { id: nextLoanId++, book: selectedBook, status:
"borrowed" }
    …
}
```

The goal is to submit a *Book* object without id and the function assigns an id for us.

So let's call it *nextBookId*. And because *library* is currently initialised with four books:

We'll start *nextBookId* at 5:

61

```
const loanQueue: Loan[] = []
let nextLoanId = 1
let nextBookId = 5
```

And in *addNewBook*, we use *nextBookId++* to increment it to the next number so the next time it runs, it's already changed. So add in **bold**:

```
function addNewBook(bookObj: Book): void {
    bookObj.id = nextBookId++;
    library.push(bookObj)
}
```

Now, let's get rid of *id* in the object we pass to *addNewBook*:

```
        Property 'id' is missing in type '{ title: string; author: string; availableCopies:
        number; }' but required in type 'Book'. ts(2345)

        index.ts(48, 5): 'id' is declared here.

        View Problem (⌥F8)    No quick fixes available
addNewBook({title: "Brave New World", author: "Aldous Huxley", availableCopies: 3 })
```

But now, TypeScript warns us that property 'id' is missing in the *Book* object. So how do we pass in a *Book* object without an id, wanting *addNewBook* to assign one for us? Could we pass in a dummy id? That wouldn't look too elegant. So how can we fix this? In the next chapter, let's address this.

Chapter 16: Utility Types – *Partial*

To address the issue in our *library* app as highlighted in the previous chapter, we're going to explore utility types. To illustrate this, we have a *Vehicle* type:

```
type Vehicle = {
    id: number
    model: string
    vehicleType: "motorcycle" | "car" | "truck"
}

const vehicles: Vehicle[] = [
    { id: 1, model: "Honda Civic", vehicleType: "car" },
    { id: 2, model: "Harley-Davidson Sportster", vehicleType:
"motorcycle" },
    { id: 3, model: "Ford F-150", vehicleType: "truck" }
];
```

This is something we've seen before. We also have an array of vehicles.
We next have a *updateVehicle* function:

```
function updateVehicle(id: number, updates: any) {

    const foundVehicle = vehicles.find(veh => veh.id === id);
    if (!foundVehicle) {
        console.error("Vehicle not found!")
        return
    }
    // Use Object.assign to update the found vehicle in place.
    Object.assign(foundVehicle, updates)
}
```

Code Explanation

```
function updateVehicle(id: number, updates: any) {
```

updateVehicle takes a number id as its first parameter. The second parameter is an object that only contain the properties we want to change. For example, we call *updateVehicle* to change only *model*:

```
updateVehicle(1, { model: "Honda Accord" });
```

Currently, *updates* is an *any* type, so that we can turn off TypeScript for now. Later, we're going to learn about utility types to type these correctly.

```
const foundVehicle = vehicles.find(veh => veh.id === id);
```

We use the *Array.find* method to get the correct vehicle based on its *id*. *find* takes a callback function, where for every vehicle we're looking through, we find the one that has the user id equal to the id passed into *updateVehicle*.

```
if (!foundVehicle) {
    console.error("Vehicle not found!")
    return
}
```

If there's no vehicle found, we say "Vehicle not found" in the console and return, so the rest of the code can't run.

```
Object.assign(foundVehicle, updates)
```

Then we use *Object.assign* so you can update the found vehicle right there. If you aren't familiar with *Object.assign*, a quick Google mentions it as:

"The *Object.assign()* static method copies all enumerable own properties from one or more source objects to a target object. It returns the modified target object."

That is, we set the *foundVehicle* as the starting object, and then replace any of the properties found in the *updates* object.

Running Our Code

Now, let's run our code with the below:

```
updateVehicle(1, { model: "Honda Accord" });
updateVehicle(3, { vehicleType: "car" } );

console.log(vehicles);
```

And we get the log:

```
(base) MacBook-Air-4:myproject user$ tsc --project ./tsconfig.json
(base) MacBook-Air-4:myproject user$ node index.js
[
  { id: 1, model: 'Honda Accord', vehicleType: 'car' },
  {
    id: 2,
    model: 'Harley-Davidson Sportster',
    vehicleType: 'motorcycle'
  },
  { id: 3, model: 'Ford F-150', vehicleType: 'car' }
]
```

If we look at vehicle with id '1', the model is now "Honda Accord".
And id '3' has the vehicle type of "car" instead of "truck".

But why are we talking about this? Well, we shouldn't be using the *any* type as mentioned previously:

```
function updateVehicle(id: number, updates: any) {…
```

However, we're not able to use *Vehicle* as our type in the parameter:

```
function updateVehicle(id: number, updates: Vehicle) {…
```

Because we're not providing a full *Vehicle* object when we don't know which property(s) is going to be passed to *updateVehicle*:

```
updateVehicle(1, { model: "Honda Accord" });
updateVehicle(3, { vehicleType: "car" } );
```

This is where the concept of Utility types can help us. Utility types can take other types as an input parameter, and then return a new type with the modifications you want. This might seem abstract now, but it will be concrete in this chapter.

In *updateVehicle*, let's use a built-in Utility type called *Partial*. The *Partial* type takes in an input you pass to it. For example, we can pass *Vehicle* type into *Partial*:

```
function updateVehicle(id: number, updates: Partial<Vehicle>) {…
```

In the above, we use the built-in type *Partial* to modify our *Vehicle* type. *Partial* then returns a new type that has all the properties of *Vehicle* set as optional (hence the name *Partial*—it contains a partial of the original properties).

Note: we use the angle bracket '<>' syntax because *Partial* uses something called Generics. You can think of *Partial* as a function, where you would normally put parentheses '{…}', but because it's a Utility type and not a function, we use angle brackets '<>' instead.

If you go ahead and hover your mouse over *Partial*, it has a type where all the properties are set as optional:

```
type Partial<T> = { [P in keyof T]?: T[P] | undefined; }
Make all properties in T optional
updates: Partial<Vehicle>) {
```

This way, we can pass an object that is missing some of the properties from a *Vehicle* object to *updateVehicle* (which takes in a partial *Vehicle* object).

65

Alternatively, you can clone a *Vehicle* type, call it *UpdateVehicle* type except that all properties are set to optional. But it would just be a lot of manual work which *Partial* Utility does for us.

You can see this in the *Partial<Type>* documentation (www.typescriptlang.org/docs/handbook/utility-types.html):

Partial<Type>

Constructs a type with all properties of Type set to optional. This utility will return a type that represents all subsets of a given type.

Released:
2.1

Example

```
interface Todo {
  title: string;
  description: string;
}

function updateTodo(todo: Todo, fieldsToUpdate: Partial<Todo>) {
  return { ...todo, ...fieldsToUpdate };
}

const todo1 = {
  title: "organize desk",
  description: "clear clutter",
};

const todo2 = updateTodo(todo1, {
  description: "throw out trash",
});
```

Try

In the documentation, you can see more examples of how *Partial* can be used.

Now, when we call *updateVehicle* with an object with only partial *Vehicle* properties, TypeScript doesn't complain anymore since the *Partial* type takes care of it.

```
updateVehicle(1, { model: "Honda Accord" });
updateVehicle(3, { vehicleType: "car" } );
```

In the next chapter, we will talk about one other utility type which relates to our Library app.

Here's the complete code used in this chapter:

```
type Vehicle = {
    id: number
    model: string
    vehicleType: "motorcycle" | "car" | "truck"
}
```

```
const vehicles: Vehicle[] = [
    { id: 1, model: "Honda Civic", vehicleType: "car" },
    { id: 2, model: "Harley-Davidson Sportster", vehicleType:
"motorcycle" },
    { id: 3, model: "Ford F-150", vehicleType: "truck" }
];

function updateVehicle(id: number, updates: Partial<Vehicle>) {

    const foundVehicle = vehicles.find(veh => veh.id === id);
    if (!foundVehicle) {
        console.error("Vehicle not found!")
        return
    }
    // Use Object.assign to update the found vehicle in place.
    Object.assign(foundVehicle, updates)
}

updateVehicle(1, { model: "Honda Accord" });
updateVehicle(3, { vehicleType: "car" } );

console.log(vehicles);
```

Chapter 17: *Omit* Utility Type

To understand the *Omit* utility type, let's create a new *addNewVehicle* function to our file from the previous chapter:

```
function addNewVehicle(newVeh: any): Vehicle {
}
```

addNewVehicle takes a new vehicle object which has all the properties of *Vehicle* except for *id* e.g.:

```
addNewVehicle({ model: "Toyota Camry", vehicleType: "car" });
```

To accommodate this, for now, we type the argument as *any*:

```
function addNewVehicle(newVeh: any): Vehicle {...
```

We will address the issue of using *any* later.

The return for *addNewVehicle* should return an *Vehicle* object that does have an id. To accommodate this, we add a *nextVehicleId* variable:

```
type Vehicle = {
    id: number
    model: string
    vehicleType: "motorcycle" | "car" | "truck"
}

let nextVehicleId = 4

const vehicles: Vehicle[] = [
    { id: 1, model: "Honda Civic", vehicleType: "car" },
    ...
];
```

We set *nextVehicleId* to 4 since there are three existing vehicles in *vehicles* array.

Let's now fill in the code for *addNewVehicle*:

```
function addNewVehicle(newVeh: any): Vehicle {
    const vehicle: Vehicle = {
        id: nextVehicleId++,
        ...newVeh
    }
    vehicles.push(vehicle)
    return vehicle
}
```

So we actually create a new vehicle object with an *id* property set to *nextVehicleId++*. With *...newVeh*, we spread all of the properties of *newVeh* into the *vehicle* object. And we push *vehicle* to the *vehicles* array.

Let's do a quick test by adding:

```
addNewVehicle({ model: "Toyota Camry", vehicleType: "car" });
```

```
console.log(vehicles);
```

When we console log, the new vehicle "Toyota Camry" should appear in *vehicles* array:

```
(base) MacBook-Air-4:myproject user$ tsc --project ./tsconfig.json
(base) MacBook-Air-4:myproject user$ node index.js
[
  { id: 1, model: 'Honda Civic', vehicleType: 'car' },
  {
    id: 2,
    model: 'Harley-Davidson Sportster',
    vehicleType: 'motorcycle'
  },
  { id: 3, model: 'Ford F-150', vehicleType: 'truck' },
  { id: 4, model: 'Toyota Camry', vehicleType: 'car' }
]
```

Be reminded that our using of *nextVehicleId++* is to simplify our illustration here, you're likely to have your database handling id assigning.

any type

Now let's address the *any* type:
```
function addNewVehicle(newVeh: any): Vehicle {...
```

Remember that with *any*, we disabled TypeScript checking and I could just add a *random* property to this object:

```
function addNewVehicle(newVeh: any): Vehicle {
    const vehicle: Vehicle = {
        id: nextVehicleId++,
        ...newVeh
    }
    vehicles.push(vehicle)
    return vehicle
}

addNewVehicle({ model: "Toyota Camry", vehicleType: "car", random:"random" });
```

And TypeScript's not going to warn us this isn't going to work even though it could create serious issues in our code. So what can we do?

70

We cannot just use the *Partial* type which turns all its properties optional. Here, we need to ensure all of the properties exist.

Here's where we can use the *Omit* type. *Omit* takes in a type (like *Partial*), but also takes a second parameter which will be a string, or union of strings.

The string(s) are the property names we want to omit from this type. And *Omit* returns a new type with the specified properties omitted. Let's take a look at the *Omit* documentation:

Omit<Type, Keys>

Constructs a type by picking all properties from `Type` and then removing `Keys` (string literal or union of string literals). The opposite of `Pick`.

Example

```typescript
interface Todo {
  title: string;
  description: string;
  completed: boolean;
  createdAt: number;
}

type TodoPreview = Omit<Todo, "description">;

const todo: TodoPreview = {
  title: "Clean room",
  completed: false,
  createdAt: 1615544252770,
};

todo;

    const todo: TodoPreview


type TodoInfo = Omit<Todo, "completed" | "createdAt">;

const todoInfo: TodoInfo = {
  title: "Pick up kids",
  description: "Kindergarten closes at 5pm",
};

todoInfo;

      const todoInfo: TodoInfo
```

(https://www.typescriptlang.org/docs/handbook/utility-types.html)

For example, in *addNewVehicle*, we can specify *Omit* like:

71

```
function addNewVehicle(newVeh: Omit<Vehicle, "id">): Vehicle {
    const vehicle: Vehicle = {
        id: nextVehicleId++,
        ...newVeh
    }
    vehicles.push(vehicle)
    return vehicle
}
```

We specify in the angle brackets '<>' *Vehicle* type in the first parameter, and in the second parameter, we specify we want to omit 'id' so the type *Omit* returns will not have *id* in it.

Omit<Vehicle,"id"> will have all the properties of *Vehicle*, just minus the *id* property. That way, *addNewVehicle* can be in charge of creating *id* for our *Vehicle* object. And now, when we have:

```
addNewVehicle({ model: "Toyota Camry", vehicleType: "car", random:"random" });
```

We get a correct warning that 'random' cannot be assigned to *Omit<Vehicle,"id">*. And if we run our code like below:

```
function addNewVehicle(newVeh: Omit<Vehicle, "id">): Vehicle {
    const vehicle: Vehicle = {
        id: nextVehicleId++,
        ...newVeh
    }
    vehicles.push(vehicle)
    return vehicle
}

addNewVehicle({ model: "Toyota Camry", vehicleType: "car" });
console.log(vehicles);
```

We can see our Toyota Camry car successfully added to *vehicles* array like before:

```
{ id: 4, model: 'Toyota Camry', vehicleType: 'car' }
```

And if we want to omit both *id* and *model*, we use the union character '|' (single pipe):
Omit<Vehicle, "id" | "model">

In this case, the input to *addNewVehicle* will just be an object with a *vehicleType* property:

addNewVehicle({ vehicleType: "car" });

Let's get back to our Library app and apply what we've learned about *Omit*.

Chapter 18: Fix TypeScript Warnings with *Omit*

Let's apply what we learned about *Omit* to our Library app's *addNewBook* function in *index*.ts:

```
function addNewBook(bookObj: Book): void {
    bookObj.id = nextBookId++;
    library.push(bookObj)
}
```

We want to provide a *Book* object has a *title, author* and *availableCopies* and function *addNewBook* will assign an id to it. So let's apply *Omit* by making the change:

```
function addNewBook(bookObj: Omit<Book,"id">): void {
    const newBook: Book = {
        id: nextBookId++,
        ...bookObj
    }
    library.push(newBook)
}
```

We use *Omit* to require the caller of `addNewBook` submit a *Book* object with all the information except for *id*.

We create a new *Book* object *newBook*, set it to an object with *id* set to *nextBookId++*, and spread in all the properties of *bookObj*. We then push *newBook* to *library*.

```
addNewBook({title: "Brave New World", author: "Aldous Huxley",
availableCopies: 3 })
```

Let's run our app. And when we console log *library*, we should have the new book added:

```
(base) MacBook-Air-4:myproject user$ tsc --project ./tsconfig.json
(base) MacBook-Air-4:myproject user$ node index.js
Library: [
  {
    id: 1,
    title: 'To Kill a Mockingbird',
    author: 'Harper Lee',
    availableCopies: 3
  },
  { id: 2, title: '1984', author: 'George Orwell', availableCopies: 2 },
  {
    id: 3,
    title: 'Pride and Prejudice',
    author: 'Jane Austen',
    availableCopies: 4
  },
  {
    id: 4,
    title: 'The Great Gatsby',
    author: 'F. Scott Fitzgerald',
    availableCopies: 2
  },
  {
    id: 5,
    title: 'Brave New World',
    author: 'Aldous Huxley',
    availableCopies: 3
  }
]
```

For the sake of this book, it isn't my objective to teach every single utility type that exists, because the documentation is straightforward. If you want to see the different types, visit: https://www.typescriptlang.org/docs/handbook/utility-types.html

But hopefully, the idea of using utility types is starting to be clearer. These utility types perform common operations on your existing types, so you don't have to do the work yourself and introduce repetitive code.

You might have noticed that Utility uses angle brackets <>. This would be a good time to talk about Generics.

Chapter 19: Generics

It's finally time to learn about Generics. Generics are a powerful tool that allows us to add flexibility to our existing types, functions, and other aspects of TypeScript code.

Similar to a function parameter which acts as a placeholder for a value you use throughout your function, a generic is a placeholder for a type you can use throughout your function. We got a taste of it when we used *Partial* and *Omit* to provide some new types in our functions. Generics will make more sense as we go through this chapter.

Generics use the angle bracket syntax '<>' (we've seen a few times already in our code). Let's look at an example, and then apply what we've learned to our Library app.

Let's create a new file generics.ts and say we have a few different arrays:

```
const bookPageCounts = [256, 320, 480, 192, 400];
const popularGenres = ["mystery", "romance", "science fiction",
"fantasy"];
const authors = [{ name: "Jane", booksPublished: 5 }, { name: "Mark",
booksPublished: 12 }];

function getLastItem(array) {
  return array[array.length - 1];
}
```

We create a simple function called *getLastItem* which takes an array as a parameter, and returns the last item of the array in JavaScript.

We can see there's a red squiggly for *array*:

Hover your mouse over *array*, and it says *array* implicitly has an *any* type. One cheater solution is to explicitly type this as an *any* type to make the warning go away:

```
function getLastItem(array: any) {
  return array[array.length - 1];
}
```

Remember that *any* type basically turns off TypeScript, and this isn't what we want. So let's remove *any* first.

The problem is, we can't say this is an array of strings, or an array of numbers, because we don't know the type. It could be an array of any item.

This is where Generics come into play. As we have mentioned, like a function has parameters that are placeholders for values, generics are a way for us to have placeholders for whatever a type is going to be.

Let's illustrate this by adding in **bold**:

```
function getLastItem<Type>(array) {
  return array[array.length - 1];
}
```

Inside our angle brackets <>, similar to how we're doing with function parameters inside parentheses, we put a placeholder for whatever type is going to be used with this function. A convention for Generics is to use the capital letter 'T' to represent type:

```
function getLastItem<T>(array) {
  return array[array.length - 1];
}
```

Remember, this is a placeholder type. The capital 'T' type here is not referring to something built into TypeScript. We could have chosen *Blah*:

```
function getLastItem<Blah>(array) {
  return array[array.length - 1];
}
```

But let's not do that and change it back to *T*.

Like in a function, we can use *T* throughout the code. We use the generic type to say that array is an array of 'T':

```
function getLastItem<T>(array: T[]) {
  return array[array.length - 1];
}
```

Remember, the name of the type doesn't matter. You can call it whatever you want as long as you're consistent throughout your code.

Let's call *getLastItem* on each of the three arrays and *console.log* the returned value so it shows in your console:

```
const bookPageCounts = [256, 320, 480, 192, 400];
const popularGenres = ["mystery", "romance", "science fiction",
"fantasy"];
const authors = [{ name: "Jane", booksPublished: 5 }, { name: "Mark",
booksPublished: 12 }];

function getLastItem<T>(array: T[]) {
    return array[array.length - 1];
}

console.log(getLastItem(bookPageCounts))
console.log(getLastItem(popularGenres))
console.log(getLastItem(authors))
```

If you hover your cursor over *bookPageCounts*:

```
                            const bookPageCounts: number[]
console.log(getLastItem(bookPageCounts))
console.log(getLastItem(popularGenres))
console.log(getLastItem(authors))
```

We can see it is typed as an array of numbers. That's inferred by TypeScript, because we didn't explicitly type it as an array of numbers.

We see the same thing with *popularGenres*, it's an array of strings:

```
console.log(getLastItem(  const popularGenres: string[]
console.log(getLastItem(popularGenres))
console.log(getLastItem(authors))
```

and with *authors*, it's an array of object literals:

```
                            const authors: {
                                name: string;
                                booksPublished: number;
console.log(getLastItem(
console.log(getLastItem(   }[]
console.log(getLastItem(authors))
```

Now hover over *getLastItem(bookPageCounts)*:

```
            function getLastItem<number>(array: number[]): number
console.log(getLastItem(bookPageCounts))
```

The type inside *getLastItem*'s angle bracket shows *number*. Then it used that *number* type to infer that the parameter *array*, is an array of *numbers*. It also inferred it returns a *number*, which we didn't explicitly state.

And if we hover over this second *getLastItem*, it does the same thing but with strings:

```
console.log(  function getLastItem<string>(array: string[]): string
console.log(getLastItem(popularGenres))
```

In the third one, it does the same thing, but with the object literal with a *name* and *booksPublished* property.

```
}            function getLastItem<{
                 name: string;
                 booksPublished: number;
             }>(array: {
                 name: string;
                 booksPublished: number;
             }[]): {
                 name: string;
console.log(     booksPublished: number;
console.log( }
console.log(getLastItem(authors))
```

Doing this allows us to write types, and functions, that can be a lot more flexible and still have some type safety without us using the *any* type, which just turns type safety off.

If you want to dive deeper into generics, you can go to the TypeScript documentation (www.typescriptlang.org/docs/handbook/2/generics.html).

getLastItem so far inferred the return type. But we can also do that explicitly by stating the generic type as our return value:

```
function getLastItem<T>(array: T[]): T{
  return array[array.length - 1];
}
```

Let's move on to the Library app and see how we might apply this to our app.

Chapter 20: Applying Generics to our Library app

In *index*.ts, currently, we have a *getBookDetail* function to find a specified book in our library array:

```
function getBookDetail(identifier: string | number): Book | undefined {
    if (typeof identifier === "string") {
        return library.find(book =>
            book.title.toLowerCase() === identifier.toLowerCase())
    } else {
        return library.find(book => book.id === identifier)
    }
}
```

Let's try to have a generic *getDetail* function which allows us to find a specified book or loan (since we don't have a *getLoanDetail* yet). Add in the below code for *getDetail*:

```
function getDetail<T>(array: T[], id: number) {
    return array.find(item => item.id === id)
}
```

To make things simpler for illustration and focus on Generics, *getDetail* will only search based on *id* (there won't be type narrowing where we allow search by id or title). And *T* in the above can represent either a *Book* type or *Loan* type.

An example usage of *getDetail* will be:
```
getDetail(library, 1)
getDetail(loanQueue, 1)
```

In the first argument, we provide the array we want to get the item from (in our case, either *library* or *loanQueue* array). In the second argument, we provide the id to search for in that array.

So with *getDetail*, there's no need for *getBookDetail* and *getLoanDetail*.

You might however notice an error with *item.id*:

```
                                    any
                        Property 'id' does not exist on type 'T'.
function getDetail<T>(array: T[], i   View Problem (⌥F8)   No quick fixes available
    // T in this case will be eithe
    return array.find(item => item.id === id)
}
```

That is, type 'T' doesn't have a property *id*. To fix this, we need to constrain the generic type *T* to ensure it has an *id* property by defining an interface:

```
interface Item {
    id: number
}
```

The *Item* interface requires an *id* of type number. And in *getDetail*, we make the below change:

```
function getDetail<T extends Item>(array: T[], id: number) {
    return array.find(item => item.id === id)
}
```

In *getDetail*, we constrain the generic type *T* to extend *Item*: <*T extends Item*>. This tells TypeScript that whatever type *T* is, it will have an *id* property of type *number*.

These changes resolve the TypeScript error while maintaining the flexibility of the generic function. Now you can use *getDetail* with any array of objects that have an id property, including both *Book*[] and *Loan*[].
And when I run my app with the code:

```
interface Item {
    id: number
}

function getDetail<T extends Item>(array: T[], id: number) {
    return array.find(item => item.id === id)
}

addNewBook({title: "Brave New World", author: "Aldous Huxley", availableCopies: 3 })
borrowBook("Brave New World")
returnBook(1)

console.log(getDetail(library, 1))
console.log(getDetail(loanQueue, 1))
```

I get the console log:

```
(base) MacBook-Air-4:myproject user$ tsc --project ./tsconfig.json
(base) MacBook-Air-4:myproject user$ node index.js
{
  id: 1,
  title: 'To Kill a Mockingbird',
  author: 'Harper Lee',
  availableCopies: 3
}
{
  id: 1,
  book: {
    id: 5,
    title: 'Brave New World',
    author: 'Aldous Huxley',
    availableCopies: 3
  },
  status: 'returned'
}
```

Which means it correctly returned both book and loan with id 1.

One last thing is, we can explicitly tell what type we are giving to *getDetail* by specifying in the angle brackets the type:

```
getDetail<Book>(library, 1)
getDetail<Loan>(loanQueue, 1)
```

This would make it clearer to other developers what you are trying to do.

Summary

We have reached the end of this introductory TypeScript book. Although we haven't covered every aspect of TypeScript, let's recap what we have learned.

We started by understanding basic, literal, and custom types in TypeScript. Then, we moved on to how to create optional properties in your typed objects.

We learned about unions and how you can combine multiple different types into a single type, which led us to learn about type narrowing. This allows us to narrow down which of those union types and edge cases we're using in our code.

We learned about some of the built-in utility types that give us extra functionality in modifying existing types in a useful way.

We capped everything off by learning about generics, which allow us to have additional flexibility in our TypeScript code.

This doesn't represent everything there is to learn about TypeScript. And I hope to add a more topics in the future.

So if you haven't already, subscribe to my mailing list at support@i-ducate.com and whenever I make a major update to this book, I'll make sure that we email out an announcement of those updates.

Hopefully, you have enjoyed this book and would like to learn more from me. I would love to get your feedback, learning what you liked and didn't for us to improve.

Please feel free to email me at support@i-ducate.com if you encounter any errors with your code or to get updated versions of this book.

If you didn't like the book, or if you feel that I should have covered certain additional topics, please email us to let us know. This book can only get better thanks to readers like you. If you like the book, I would appreciate if you could leave us a review too. Thank you and all the best!

About the Author

Greg Lim is a technologist and author of several programming books. Greg has many years in teaching programming in tertiary institutions and he places special emphasis on learning by doing.

Contact Greg at support@i-ducate.com